I SPY
Halloween Book
For Kids Ages 2-5

Copyright 2020 by Happy Harper - All rights reserved.

This document is geared towards providing exact and reliable information in regards to the topic and issue covered. The publication is sold with the idea that the publisher is not required to render an accounting, officially permitted, or otherwise, qualified services. If advice is necessary, legal or professional, a practiced individual in the profession should be ordered.

- From a Declaration of Principles which was accepted and approved equally by a Committee of the American Bar Association and a Committee of Publishers and Associations.

In no way is it legal to reproduce, duplicate, or transmit any part of this document by either electronic means or in printed format. Recording of this publication is strictly prohibited and any storage of this document is not allowed unless with written permission from the publisher. All rights reserved.

The information provided herein is stated to be truthful and consistent, in that any liability, in terms of inattention or otherwise, by any usage or abuse of any policies, processes, or directions contained within is the solitary and utter responsibility of the recipient reader. Under no circumstances will any legal responsibility or blame be held against the publisher for any reparation, damages, or monetary loss due to the information herein, either directly or indirectly.

Respective authors and companies own all copyrights not held by the publisher.

The information herein is offered for informational purposes solely and is universal as so. The presentation of the information is without a contract or any type of guarantee assurance.

The trademarks that are used are without any consent, and the publication of the trademark is without permission or backing by the trademark owner. All trademarks and brands within this book are for clarifying purposes only and are owned by the owners themselves, not affiliated with this document.

THIS BOOK BELONGS TO

SPOOOOKY HINT...
ALL THE PAGES CAN BE COLORED IN FOR EXTRA FUN!

I SPY WITH MY LITTLE EYE SOMETHING STARTING WITH THE LETTER

I SPY WITH MY LITTLE EYE SOMETHING STARTING WITH THE LETTER

I SPY WITH MY LITTLE EYE SOMETHING STARTING WITH THE LETTER

I SPY WITH MY LITTLE EYE SOMETHING STARTING WITH THE LETTER

I SPY WITH MY LITTLE EYE SOMETHING STARTING WITH THE LETTER

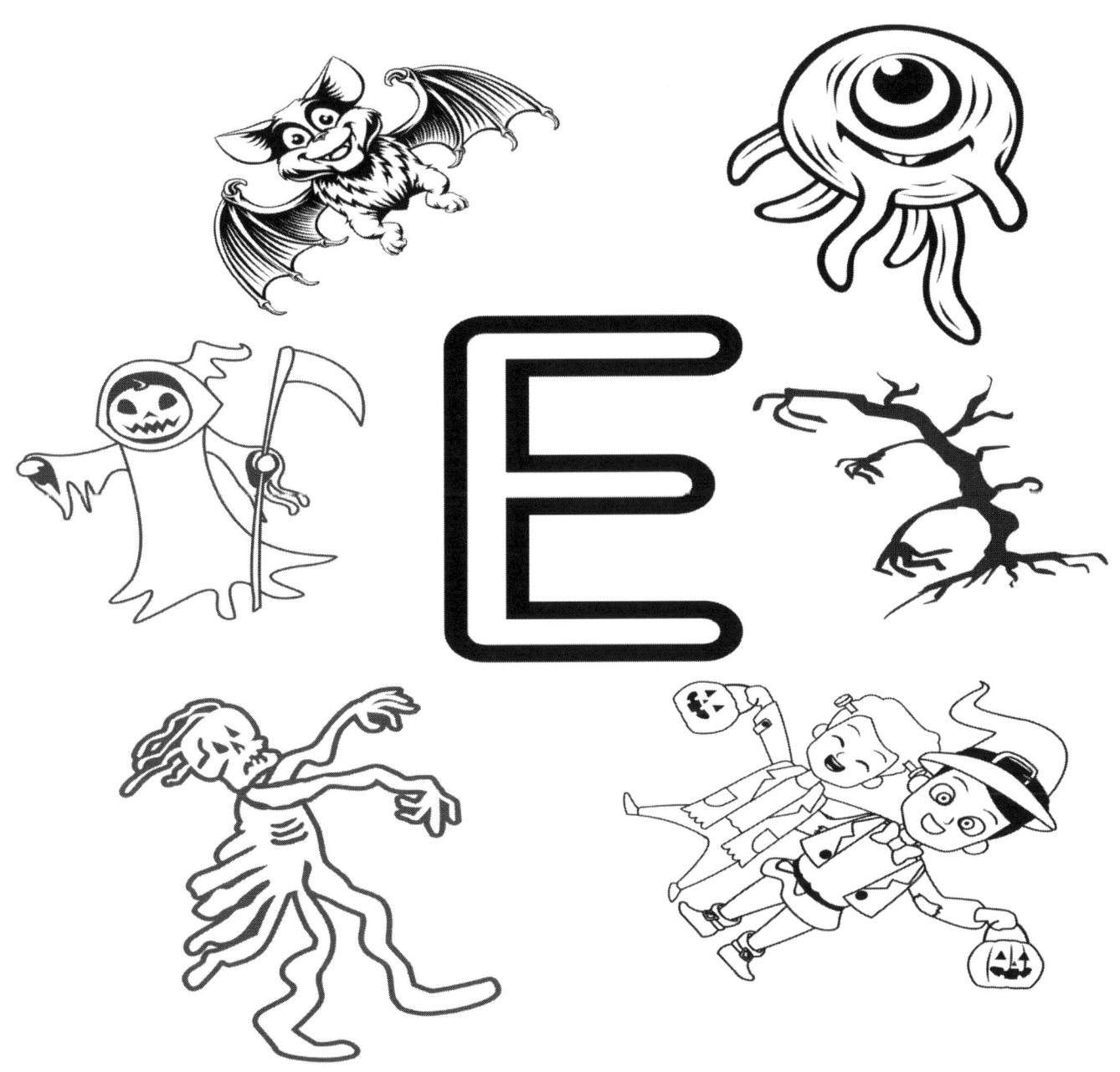

I SPY WITH MY LITTLE EYE SOMETHING STARTING WITH THE LETTER

I SPY WITH MY LITTLE EYE SOMETHING STARTING WITH THE LETTER

I SPY WITH MY LITTLE EYE SOMETHING STARTING WITH THE LETTER

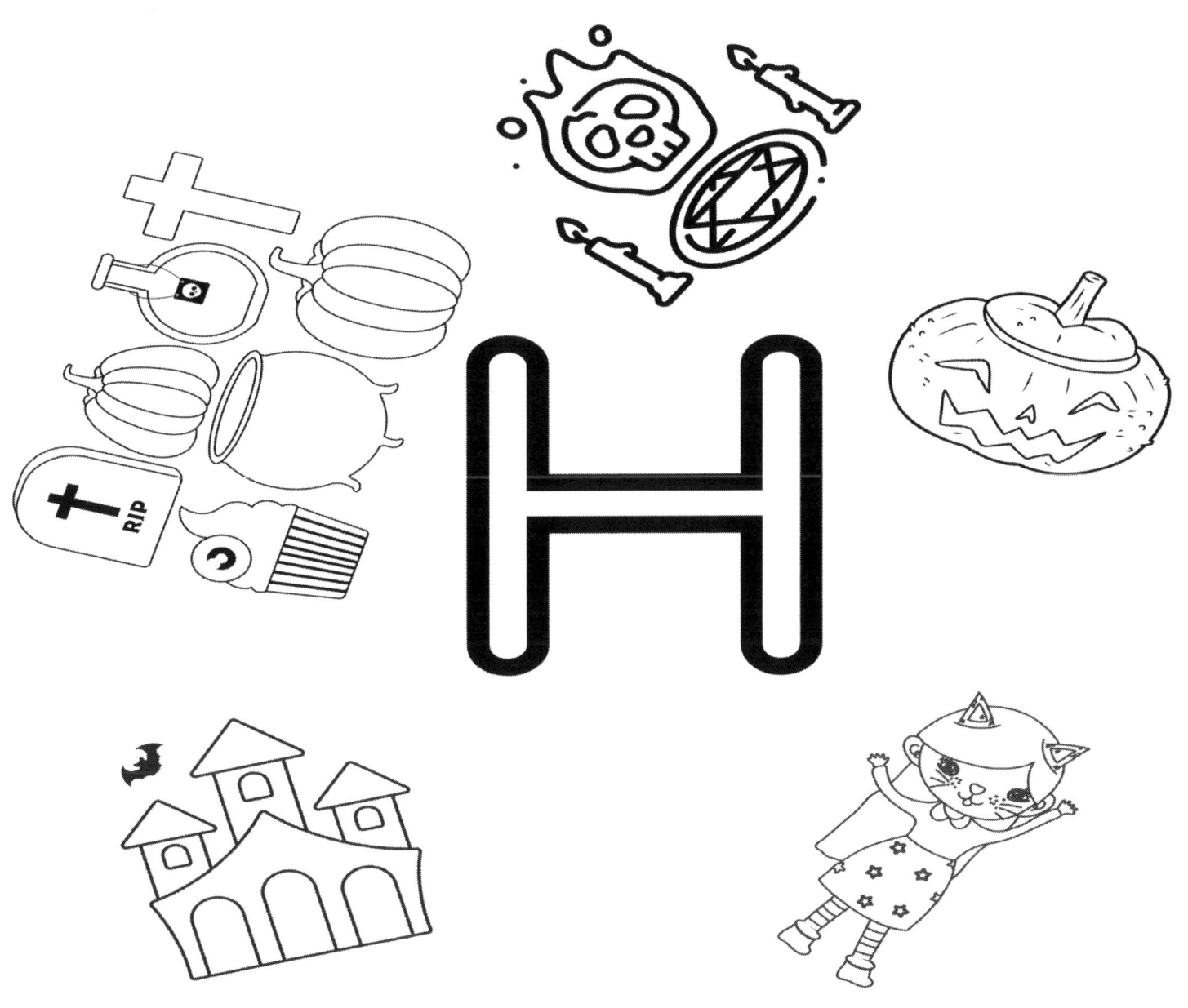

I SPY WITH MY LITTLE EYE SOMETHING STARTING WITH THE LETTER

I SPY WITH MY LITTLE EYE SOMETHING STARTING WITH THE LETTER

ENJOYING THE BOOK? PLEASE LEAVE A REVIEW AND LET US KNOW!

I SPY WITH MY LITTLE EYE SOMETHING STARTING WITH THE LETTER

I SPY WITH MY LITTLE EYE SOMETHING STARTING WITH THE LETTER

I SPY WITH MY LITTLE EYE SOMETHING STARTING WITH THE LETTER

I SPY WITH MY LITTLE EYE SOMETHING STARTING WITH THE LETTER

I SPY WITH MY LITTLE EYE SOMETHING STARTING WITH THE LETTER

I SPY WITH MY LITTLE EYE SOMETHING STARTING WITH THE LETTER

I SPY WITH MY LITTLE EYE SOMETHING STARTING WITH THE LETTER

I SPY WITH MY LITTLE EYE SOMETHING STARTING WITH THE LETTER

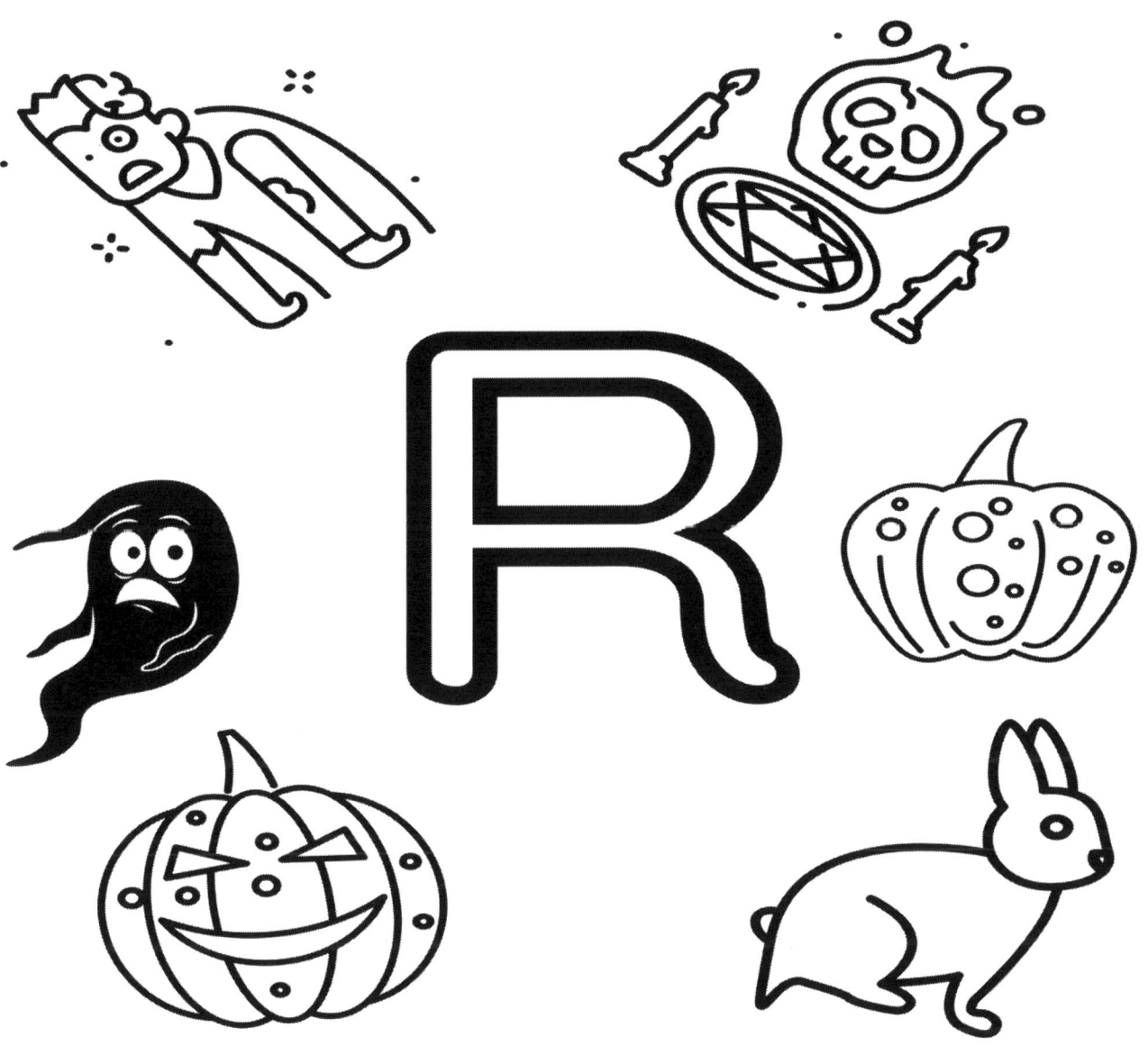

I SPY WITH MY LITTLE EYE SOMETHING STARTING WITH THE LETTER

I SPY WITH MY LITTLE EYE SOMETHING STARTING WITH THE LETTER

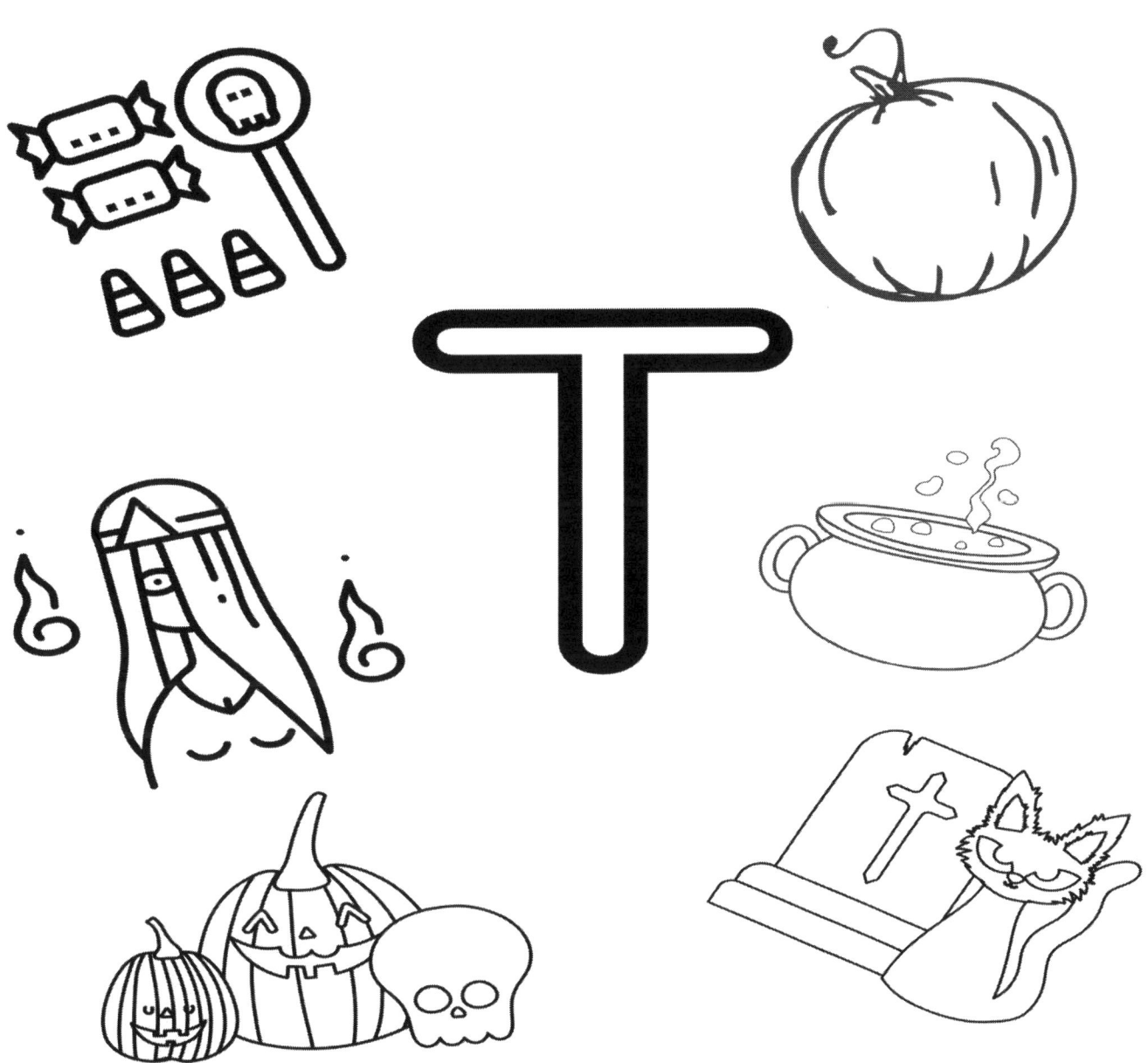

I SPY WITH MY LITTLE EYE SOMETHING STARTING WITH THE LETTER

I SPY WITH MY LITTLE EYE SOMETHING STARTING WITH THE LETTER

I SPY WITH MY LITTLE EYE SOMETHING STARTING WITH THE LETTER

I SPY WITH MY LITTLE EYE SOMETHING STARTING WITH THE LETTER

I SPY WITH MY LITTLE EYE SOMETHING STARTING WITH THE LETTER

I SPY WITH MY LITTLE EYE SOMETHING STARTING WITH THE LETTER

CONGRATULATIONS ON GETTING THROUGH THE ALPHABET!

IF YOU ENJOYED THIS ACTIVITY BOOK, PLEASE LEAVE A REVIEW AND LET US KNOW WHAT YOU LIKED THE MOST!

YOU CAN FIND THE ALL THE I SPY ANSWERS AT THE BACK!

AS A THANK YOU FOR PURCHASING THIS BOOK, ENJOY THESE BONUS COLORING PAGES FROM ONE OF OUR COLORING BOOKS!

BE SURE TO CHECK OUT ALL OF OUR OTHER COLORING BOOKS AND ACTIVITY BOOKS BY TYPING IN "HAPPY HARPER COLORING FOR KIDS" OR "HAPPY HARPER ACTIVITY FOR KIDS" ON AMAZON!

A IS FOR APPLE

B IS FOR BAT

C IS FOR CAT

D IS FOR DRAGON

E IS FOR EYEBALL

F IS FOR FROG

G IS FOR GHOST

H IS FOR HAUNTED HOUSE

I IS FOR IGLOO

J IS FOR JOKER

K IS FOR KITE

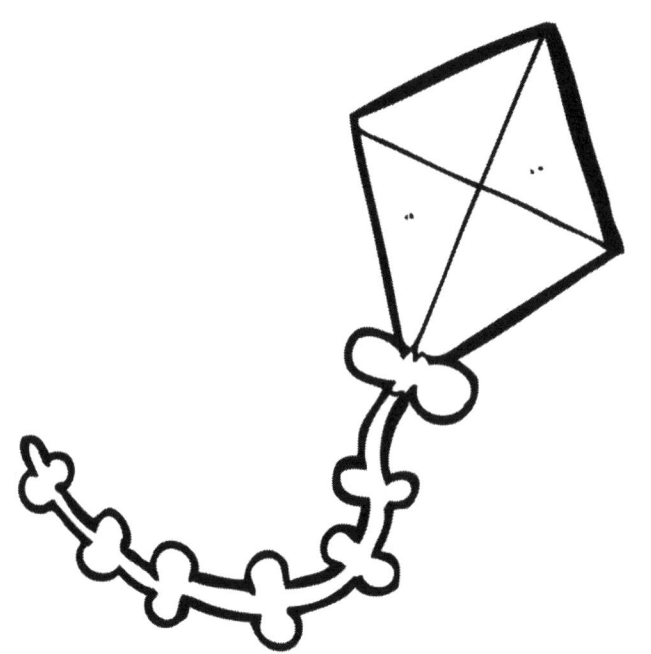

L IS FOR LION

M IS FOR MOON

N IS FOR NEST

O IS FOR OWL

P IS FOR PENGUIN

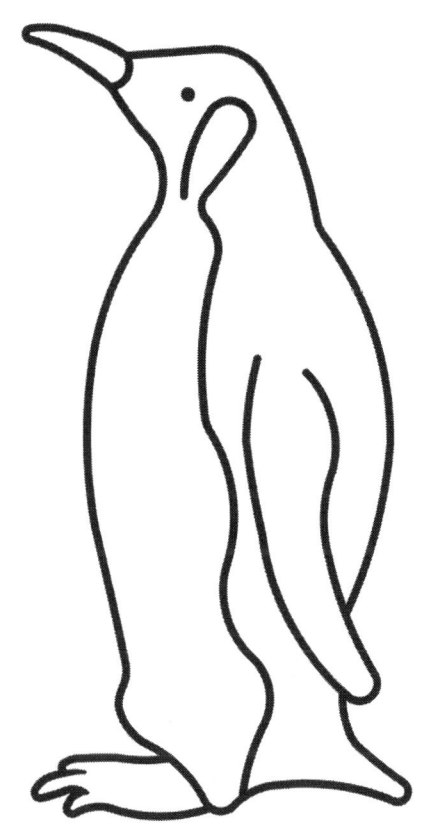

Q IS FOR QUEEN

R IS FOR RABBIT

S IS FOR SKELETON

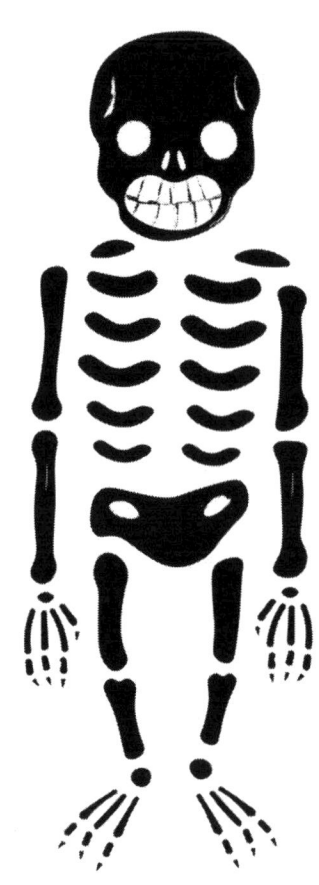

T IS FOR TREAT

U IS FOR UNICORN

V IS FOR VAMPIRE

W IS FOR WITCH

X IS FOR XYLOPHONE

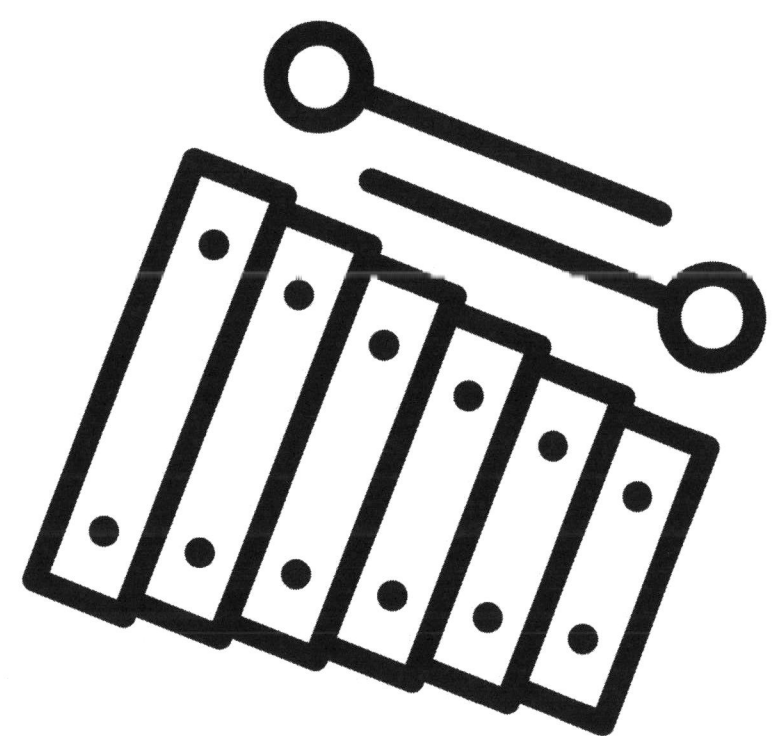

Y IS FOR YAK

Z IS FOR ZOMBIE

HAPPY HALLOWEEN!

Manufactured by Amazon.ca
Bolton, ON